WE HAD PRAYIN' MOTHERS

DR. NEAL ROBINSON

978-1-7355883-4-6 (Print)

978-1-7355883-5-3 (Ebook)

Printed in the United States of America

DEDICATION

I dedicate this book to Michael's mother Lou and my mother Janet whose prayers surrounded us with protective angels in so many challenging and dangerous situations, and to my wife Elaine and our son Ryan who, along with my mother, encouraged me to write it.

"Listen, my son! Listen, son of my womb! Listen, my son, the answer to my prayers!"

PROVERBS 31:2 NIV

INTRODUCTION

When we started out on this amazing adventure in 1974, we were just 19 years old and full of ourselves. As the years passed, I thought of it as a personal achievement, a measure of my own strength. I was a self-confessed atheist and continued to be so until I received Jesus into my life in 2005. I was raised in the Methodist Church but had come to know Christianity as a religion and not the relationship that it should be. I have come to know that this adventure was a victory and example of the power of prayer, our mothers' prayers in this case. Is there an unsaved person who needs your prayers today? Your prayers could make a tremendous difference, even an amazing victory in their life!

Ten Speeds, Pannier Bags, and the Open Road

Trouble seems to always starts with a girl, especially when you're a boy in college. While some details from the 70's are foggy for many reasons, my conversation with Pamela is not. It was 1974 and I was 19 years old with two years of college at West Valley College in Saratoga, California under my belt. I was a bit of an adventurer and thrill seeker you could say. I was known to go hiking in the local Santa Cruz Mountains, and also in the wilderness areas of the High Sierra Mountains. I also had a small motorcycle back then which I enjoyed riding along the California railroad just to explore.

Pamela was a close friend from school. The most attractive close "friend" I had. One day we were talking about life and adventures and she planted a seed into my impressionable lizard brain. She admired my spirit for adventure and knew I liked to ride along the railroad so she suggested that I go beyond the local town and follow the tracks across the country to see where they would lead me. I naturally thought that was a brilliant idea, and I'm sure I wasn't trying to impress her either. The idea became an obsession. I roped my friend Michael into joining me but I don't remember exactly how. Of course, he wasn't nearly as cute as Pamela so that's understandable, I suppose.

Michael and I had known each other since junior high school and lived in the same general area, walking distance to school. During those years, I worked as a newspaper carrier for The San Jose Mercury and would rise at four o'clock in the morning every day to fold and deliver newspapers on my bicycle and saddle bags in a hilly neighborhood.

Out of high school, I was accepted to Fresno State University but decided to attend West Valley Junior College instead. I am glad that I decided not to. How different my life's direction would have been if I had gone to Fresno. But after a very busy two years of making movies and participating in track and the fencing team, I was ready to see the country and Michael was too. However, Michael did not have a motorcycle so we had to improvise and decided that we would circumnavigate the United States on ten speed bicycles.

While Michael and I were close friends and both loved adventures, we were different in many ways. I was driven, focused, and highly disciplined while Michael was more relaxed, laid back, and an artistic type. We never once considered how this might affect our approach to accomplishing our goal, we were just excited to go explore our beautiful country.

The route seemed simple enough to us. We would head south down the California coast, cross the Southwest and head to Florida, then continue up the east coast, and back west along the northern states, and finally return down the western coast to California. Sounds great, doesn't it?

This adventure of course required some funding. Thankfully, while attending West Valley Junior College, I worked a summer job at a catering park called Blackberry Farms where I parked cars, shucked corn, raked leaves, and picked up trash. On evenings and weekends during the school year I worked at a coffee house called "The Upstart Crow." I managed to save enough money to buy equipment for the trip and had enough left over to start out with six hundred dollars in traveler's checks in my pocket.

We ordered Raleigh brand ten speed touring bicycles at a local bike shop, and then started accumulating the gear we would need to make the ride. These bikes had extra wide handlebars to accommodate a storage bag. Over the rear wheel on a frame would hang saddle bags, called pannier bags that had two side compartments and a top compartment. We would also carry small backpacks. Because I had participated in several long backpacking trips in the High Sierra Nevada Mountains while in high school. I was familiar with camping equipment and knew all the army surplus stores in the Bay Area which were a good source for affordable camping gear. We planned to cook all of our meals along the way, so we bought a small white gas camp stove and a light aluminum pot and skillet. We would learn later that the stove was tricky to light and control, but it all seemed like a solid plan from the start. We also purchased a White Stag brand, two-man tent that had a zip up screen door, window, and a rain fly, plus it was light weight. With practice, we could set up quickly. One of our best finds was the four-pound goose down sleeping bags that never failed to keep one warm, as long as we kept them dry. We made sure to bring light plastic tarps to cover them while riding in the rain.

Obviously, space was limited and the weight concerns were real. It was a challenge to decide what to take and what not to take. We would be crossing the great deserts of the southwest in the fall and temperatures would be dropping, especially at the higher elevations. The concept of layering would prove to work well. Long underwear, a couple of t-shirts, two wool sweaters (made by my mother), an Adidas warm up suit, running shorts, cotton athletic socks, and a pair of heavy wool socks was all that I would bring. I also bought an army surplus pair of rip-stop cotton jungle pants.

With the panniers loaded with clothes, I would strap my sleeping bag and the tent on top of my bike and Mike would strap his sleeping bag and his violin case on top of his. We knew music would be a perk along the way and Mike was, and is, an accomplished fiddle player and so it came with us. It added a lot to our trip and slowed us down at times too!

The Ride Begins

We set out on a morning in September from my parents' home in Los Gatos. I am sure that neither one of us got much sleep that night. Mom and dad woke up early to send us off. They thought we were a little crazy but knew we had our minds made up. Dad was an ex-marine and not the "touchy feely" type. He predicted we'd be back in three days. Mom was a hard worker and somewhat stoic herself. If she was worried, she did not show it. Raising four boys, I was the oldest, while moving all over the country during the 1960's had been a challenge. I think that she had more confidence in me than my father did. She took photos of us and insisted I call as often as I could, which would mean finding payphones along the route. Not exactly a priority on my list.

We headed out and planned to meet a group of our friends at Manresa Beach just south of Santa

Cruz later that evening. This would mean crossing the Santa Cruz Mountains that day, which was a bold start. We had trained in these mountains, but not with our bikes loaded with all that gear. We were both carrying sixty or seventy pounds of gear, depending on how much food we had with us. This took some planning, which we got used to. We had found some good simple recipes for breakfasts and dinners. Typically, we would have canned goods like chili and roast beef hash. Eggs, powdered milk, baking mix, potatoes, and onions were also on board. The added weight made hill climbing more challenging and going downhill like rocket flight! Our riding skills were sharpened along the way, starting on that first day.

Highway 17 was the main route from Los Gatos to Santa Cruz, but cyclists were not allowed on it. We chose to ride a trail up Los Gatos Creek that led up to the Lexington Dam. There we joined up with the Old Santa Cruz Highway which took us to Summit Road. We turned south on that road and then turned towards the coast on Soquel-San Jose Road, reaching Manresa Beach in the late afternoon, having traveled forty miles through mountainous terrain. A group of close friends met us there for a bonfire and a late night of celebration. Not so early the next morning we headed south towards Monterey. We would take every day as it came, not knowing how far we would ride or where the next camp would be. Every day was an adventure.

The next evening, after riding just 32 miles due to our late start, we were nearing the campus of Monterrey Peninsula College and as we thought about where to stop, that seemed like as good a place as any. We figured we could inconspicuously set up camp near a large, park like area of dry grass and trees on the campus and hopefully head out early the next morning undetected. There were also open showers available there. Posing as students, we were able to clean up. It would be a few days before that would happen again.

In the morning we went about making breakfast. The little white gas stove we had purchased was difficult to light and control. This was our first time to use it and our inexperience with it led to some excitement that morning. The stove required pumping and priming with a little fuel. As I fumbled around trying to light it, some fuel spilled, and the stove tipped over which started the dry grass on fire! The fire was quickly spreading and in a panic, we furiously stomped like two fellas in River Dance. Many choice expletives were uttered as we danced. I don't know how, but with great relief we finally got the fire out! A large cloud of smoke drifted towards the main buildings on campus. This caught the attention of a security guard who motored over to us on a small trail bike. He was a big man in uniform, much bigger than his bike, which was a silly sight and we tried not to snicker as he approached. He made sure that we knew that camping was not allowed on the campus and he was not happy that our breakfast fire had happened. We assured him that we were leaving right away, and then did!

So much for being inconspicuous, and thank God for prayin' mothers.

Big Sur And The Coastal Highway

Highway 1 curls up and down through the cliffs and beaches of Big Sur which was dead ahead. Big Sur is 71 miles of rugged coastline and was going to strengthen our cycling legs quickly. Steep climbs and super-fast descents combined with hairpin turns made this road a real roller coaster. I had experienced this route once before when my father had driven us to San Simeon to visit Hearst Castle, but this was a completely different experience. This was not for the faint of heart, and my heart was often in my mouth as I tightly gripped my handlebars in the effort to maintain control. Heading south put us on the cliff side of this two-lane highway, and there was usually no guardrail. Little or no shoulder left no room for mistakes and large trucks were common. Plummeting downhill with our weight-enhanced inertia left our brakes somewhat useless. The Pacific Ocean crashed against the rocks often hundreds of feet below with the cliff just a few feet away on the right. This required focus. The beauty was terrifyingly incredible.

Evening was upon us and it was time to look for a suitable camping spot again. Jumping a fence, we settled down in a forested area on the downhill side and set up our tent and hunkered down for the night. Sometime in the predawn darkness, we were awoken by the sound of our tent unzipping followed by the blinding light of a flashlight in our faces, along with the "business end" of a two barrel shotgun. We found out the hard way that camping on the private property of the Esalen Institute was not allowed. There was no argument from us--we broke camp and moved on just as the sun was rising.

Undeterred and resolute, we continued south on the Coast Highway 1, finding a campground in San Simeon some 80 miles south of Monterrey which had running water. Highway 1 moved inland where it joined Highway 101 at San Luis Obispo. Together then they returned to the coast. We stopped for the night at Pismo Beach where there were public showers. I remember how friends loved to go there for weekend camping trips.

We were experiencing a way of traveling that is so different from automobile road trips. In a car you are insulated from the winds, from the smells, from the rise and fall of the terrain, and from the sounds of the road. On a bicycle you experience it all.

Highway 1 left 101 at Arroyo Grande and then went south past Vandenberg Air Force Base to Lompoc. It was just before Lompoc that I had my first mechanical malfunction. My freewheel, the part of the bicycle that the pedals are attached to that allows the wheels to turn when not pedaling, decided to seize up. How in the world was I going to replace it? We were in an agricultural area. It was highly unlikely that we would find a bicycle shop around there. We came across a mower and tractor supply store right out in the middle of nowhere and went inside to see if anyone knew how far the next bike shop was. As angels would have it, they actually did bicycle repair there and they had the proper part. In no time, I was good to go! What are the chances? Very slim. Unless you had a prayin' mother.

We camped just outside of Lompoc in a pasture off Highway 246 which would take us inland the next day to Buellton. There we found the famous Andersen's Pea Soup Restaurant. It was all you could eat soup and by that time, we could eat a lot of soup, and so we did! So much so that we had to find somewhere to camp nearby. Too much pea soup can lead to some gastric distress, as we learned.

There was no thought of us turning back as my father had predicted. We were well past his 3-day prediction. The next day we would take on one of the most difficult rides yet. Highway 154 would take us to Santa Barbara where we planned to stay for a few days with my brother Phillip, who was attending the University of California there. In between us and him were the Santa Inez Mountains. Hwy 154 crossed these mountains over the San Marcos pass. This was an old stagecoach route, and many of them were lost on that treacherous trail. We had no idea what lay ahead when we started out that morning. The twisting, tortuous road climbs thousands of feet before descending to Santa Barbara. Our bike pedals were outfitted with toe clips which held our feet to the pedals. This allowed the ascending pedal to be pulled up as the descending pedal was being pushed down. The result was an increase in available power. Without them, the mountain pass would have been unclimbable, even in the lowest gear. We spent most of that day climbing San Marcos Pass in the lowest gear. The miles crawled by. That climb seemed to last forever. The descent into Santa Barbara was glorious and quick.

My brother, Phillip, had been expecting us. There was excitement in the air about our expedition and arrival. We were treated like celebrities. Staying at the University of Santa Barbara was like being at a resort. Phillip and his roommate hosted us in their room in the Anacapa Dormitory. They gave us their entry cards for the dining hall and the food was good and plenty. I remember hearing that there were three girls for every boy on that campus, and it seemed to be true. The dorm building was right on the beach and there were large grass common areas that were perfect for throwing Frisbees, which was one of my favorite sports. I have a warm memory of throwing the disk with a group of people, mostly girls, out on the sunny commons while The Allman Brothers' song "Jessica" played in the background. It was perfect. We were invited to parties in Goleta, the small university town, and were entertained as well as any college kid in our day could dream.

Then it was time to go. The great deserts of the Southwest lay ahead. We were careful to avoid the heat of summer, but we also wanted to avoid winter snows while crossing the high deserts and the Great Divide. We continued south on Highway 1 toward Los Angeles.

Unspoken Rules of the Road

For safety reasons, we chose not to ride in darkness. The eighteen-wheel tractor-trailer trucks would blow by us on the highway, requiring us to have a steady grip and balance on often irregular surfaces. The highway shoulder to the right was our space to ride in. At times, it was a generous space, as much as four or five feet and smooth, at times it would be nearly nothing with broken and irregular pavement. We always rode in tandem, never shoulder to shoulder. The lead rider created a wind break for the following rider, and we would trade positions frequently. This maximized our energy and helped us ride for long periods of time. I regret that, due to my aggressive nature, sometimes I would bump Michael's rear tire when I was the follower and would outpace him when I was the leader. I knew that this was frustrating for him and I tried to do better but my pedal to the metal nature would push through from time to time.

With just a few inches to ride on, and often a precipitous drop just to your right, continued focus was imperative. When the big rigs would blast by at highway speeds of 80 mph or more, the cab portion passing would produce a wind wave that shoved you to the right. Then the gap between the cab and the trailer drew you back to the left quickly. Just as quickly, a blast of air created by the trailer would throw you back to the right. We got used to this, but you had to keep your head about you as we often rode from 6 to 8 hours a day. The shoulder could also offer other surprises. A coiled rattlesnake sunning itself on the pavement had us raising our feet quickly up high off the pedals. Tarantula spiders that run the desert in herds were smashed by our tires, and thousands more by the big rigs. Road kills had to be swerved around, and the stench had you holding your breath as long as you could! The incredible views that we encountered were more than enough to make up for those moments. Traveling by bicycle gives one an appreciation for the countryside that motored vehicle travel cannot come close to. As we made our way across the country, long haul truck drivers who had passed us days earlier would recognize us and honk their horns at us on their return trip.

The most important guidance of the sun was sundown. It was important to keep an eye on the setting sun and the terrain in order to find a suitable camp site and have enough time to set up the tent before dark. Using any kind of lantern would have defeated our need for remaining inconspicuous. We found out that there was an art to setting up the tent. We had brought thin foam pads that served as insulation under our sleeping bags but did not provide much padding and support for our tired frames. We learned how to scratch out depressions in the hard ground that would accommodate our shoulders and hips, but this had to be done before the tent was laid down, and we had to be watchful for ant colonies as well. Most of the time there was not a mound but just a hole in the ground that they would stream in and out of. If we found any that were near our tent site, we would pour a little camp fuel down the hole and torch them. Fortunately, our White Stag tent had good zip up doors, windows, and screens that kept most of the other insects out. Many of the desert ants were big black monsters that would bite the hell out of you. The tent also had a rain fly which was a staked-out covering over the roof of the tent that provided additional water proofing, stability, and insulation. This tent proved its worth many times through wind and rain, and as a barrier to wild animals such as snakes, javelina, tarantulas, and God knows what else in the middle of the night.

Ventura Highway

Michael and I had become accustomed to life on the road and the daily process of searching out a place to stop each night. However, I was determined to ride as many miles as possible each day and Michael was determined to enjoy each stop. He was not an early riser like I was and he enjoyed taking his time in the morning. This led to some friction at times as I was always pushing to break camp and get going. When he would stop to rosin up his bow in the morning, I knew that we would have a late start.

We continued south along the Coastal Highway, passing through Ventura and Oxnard. Between Santa Barbara and Ventura, the highway was right on the ocean. We had the beach on our right and the mountains on our left. It was overwhelmingly majestic in every direction. We passed through small beach towns that were busy with tourists and surfers. The terrain was level and we made good time. It was a very picturesque and enjoyable part of the ride. At Ventura, the highway turned inland to Oxnard, where Highway 1 leaves 101 and returns to the ocean, passing through Naval Base Point Mugu. I remembered visiting there with my parents to see an air show when we lived in LA in the 1960's. Continuing down the Pacific Coast on Hwy 1 was a relatively easy and fun ride. The terrain was mostly level and the view of the ocean was wonderful. We made good time and camping areas were readily available.

When we reached Santa Monica, we turned inland on Wilshire Blvd. and headed toward Hollywood, stopping to visit with my grandparents who gifted me with a small battery-operated transistor radio. This was to come in very handy later. I mounted it on my handlebars to listen to music and weather reports. I remember hearing Carol King's new hit "Jazzman" and "Ventura Highway" by America as we rode along. While in Hollywood we stayed with a college friend who was enrolled in a music school there. He was a talented musician who had helped us with the soundtrack of our last film. We stayed in his apartment for a couple of days and saw the stars on Hollywood Boulevard. One evening we came across a free concert in a local park. It was a folk music concert featuring Will Gere whom we found out had been a contemporary of legendary folk singer Woody Guthrie.

Saying goodbye to our friend, we left Hollywood

and headed south toward Anaheim where Michael had family. Making our way along the Imperial Highway, we passed through the neighborhood of Watts. We were aware that this could possibly be a dangerous area as there had been racial strife here in the sixties. As we continued along the Imperial Highway, an African American man wearing sunglasses and riding a chopped stingray bicycle rode along beside us for a short way. This was a bike with the long banana seat down low and the handlebars up high. He asked us while we pedaled along where we were from. When we explained that we had ridden from San Francisco he exclaimed, "How come you ain't on the news?" He also declared that we must have "balls a foot wide" which we naturally took as a huge compliment. Later on in the trip, I think it was in Texas, a fellow declared that we must have "cast iron balls" but I am pretty sure that having cast iron balls a foot wide would have slowed us down a lot.

We stayed several days in Anaheim where we did some maintenance on our bikes. Michael's family was very welcoming and generous. Back in the saddle, we returned to the Pacific Coast Highway and headed south towards San Diego. As before, the ride along the Pacific was mild and picturesque. Our next destination was the University of California at San Diego, which was in La Jolla. We had some friends attending there. We stayed with them in the dorms, which were just as nice as those that we stayed in at UCSB. The food, and the girls, were just as nice too! Riding around La Jolla and into San Diego for a couple of days gave us some good hill climb training, which we had not had much of since Big Sur and San Marcos Pass. We had been having an easy ride for a while with frequent rest, good food, and relaxation. All of that was about to change.

Go East

We didn't know it but the serious part of our adventure was about to begin. There would not be another real rest break until we reached Houston, Texas 1,600 miles away. We packed up, mounted up, and headed northwest into the San Diego Mountains. It was already October, so we were going to miss the hottest part of the year in the deserts, but we had to get a move on in order not to get caught in the heavy winter of the high plains. Fortunately, we were somewhat prepared for winter. I had those close-knit wool sweaters that my mother had made for me and we had our goose down sleeping bags that were very efficient. The cold was to come much sooner than we anticipated.

We left UCSD and headed east into the San Diego Mountains. At Poway we had gone 20 miles and climbed just 500 feet. The town of Julian was on the summit that we were headed for. That left us 47 miles and nearly 4000 feet left to climb. The weather was beginning to change and it was getting cloudy and cooler. We turned right on Poway Road and headed uphill toward Ramona. Somewhere near Ramona it was beginning to rain, so we decided to make camp next to the highway. It was a cold rain. We were determined not to let our things get wet, so we quickly set up our tent and covered our bikes and packs with tarps. This was the first inclement weather that we had encountered on our journey. We knew that letting our clothing and sleeping bags get soaked with cold water would be a disaster. It rained all night and through the next day, and the temperature continued to drop. Fortunately, we had brought enough food with us from the UCSD commons to sustain us without having to go outside and cook. Laying in a small two-man tent for more than a day was no fun. We were fortunate that no one bothered us as our tent was close to the highway and could easily be seen. The following day we decided that we needed to continue. The rain had lightened, but it was still cold. The radio told us that snow was possible, so we knew that we should press on to make the summit at Julian. That meant another 3000 feet of climbing over nearly 30 miles. We protected our gear with tarps and rode on.

We were not new to hill climbing. Big Sur had been a hard teacher in that regard. But the climbing this time was different. Hwy 1 through Big Sur was a series of steep climbs and glorious downhill runs. In contrast, this was a never-ending climb, similar to our San Marcos Pass climb but longer and much colder. Much of the time, depending on the severity of the grade, we would be in our lowest gear. That involves the smallest gear on the front sprocket and the largest one on the back sprocket, which provides the mechanical advantage. You put your head down and keep pumping and pulling, making sure to use as much ankle flexion and extension as possible. If for some reason you must stop, getting back on and going is very difficult.

Our progress was slow. We had to get to Julian before dark and had no idea if we would find a place to camp there. The only information source that we had was a paper map. The cold rain was sinking in and our energy was decreasing. Exhausted, we rode into Julian late in the day and stopped at a gas station to ask about camping. Michael was clearly depleted and shaking, and so was I. The man working the service station decided that he did not like our looks and asked us to leave. Probably because we had not shaven since we left the Bay Area, and our hair was getting longer. Fortunately, someone outside told us that there was a group of small cabins nearby that we could rent daily for a small amount so we reserved one for the night. This was a miracle! It had a wood burning stove, which was pure luxury. We were able to dry out our gear and warm up our shivering bodies. A hot meal was truly appreciated as we watched it snow out the window all night. We were only 60 miles from balmy San Diego. I'm convinced, our mothers' prayers got us there.

The next morning, we were dry and rested and somewhat refreshed. The reward for a long bicycle climb is the exhilarating descent down the other side. That day, we plunged over 4000 feet from Julian to the Colorado Desert town of Ocotillo Wells just 33 miles away. In doing so we passed through the beautiful Anza Borrego Desert State Park. This would be one of the most memorable days of riding for us. We started in a frosted mountain pine forest and by the end of the day were rolling along a desert highway. The grand scenery whisked by and the weather had become almost perfect. The colors of the brush and cactus there were shades of green, yellow, orange, and red. I remember a beautiful red fox running across the road in front of us. We stopped at a small store near a camping area for water and some canned food and then continued on. We were officially in the desert and would be for many miles to come.

Desert Life

There were things that we learned about camping in the desert, some things we wished we hadn't. There were no highway rest stops, few camping grounds, and the distance between towns could be great. Because water is heavy, we could not carry much and had to plan accordingly. We both carried a half gallon plastic jug of water, as well as a pint bottle on the bike frame for water breaks during the day. Break downs were bound to happen. There was cactus that would break off in pieces and the spiny limbs could blow out on the highway and puncture tires. A flat tire or a broken spoke could leave you camped prematurely. We had to make sure that our water supplies were topped off as often as possible. We also learned to clean our cooking gear with sand instead of water.

Tumble Weeds

From Ocotillo Wells to Brawley was 40 miles with an elevation change bringing us over 100 feet below sea level. The terrain was flat desert and very dry. Hwy 78 took us just a mile from the Salton Sea. We could not see it, but we could smell the salty water. Fortunately, the weather was temperate. From there to the east of Brawley was an agricultural area. This land is very hot in the summer, well over 100 degrees during the day. The desert ground is hard and rocky. This kind of terrain made it difficult to hide our camping places and there certainly weren't any phone booths. There was usually a fence to climb, and not very much foliage other than tumble weeds to hide behind. Large rocks occasionally offered cover. East of Brawley we found a large sand desert. There were sand dunes stretching to the horizon, and a small park not far from Highway 78 where we camped. I remember seeing the trails left by critters. Tarantulas and snakes left their tracks in the sand. The sand was far more comfortable to lay on than the hard scrabble desert but the hard desert would return the next day.

Hwy 78 turned to the north, and the Chocolate Mountains were on the left horizon. They are aptly named. These desert mountains were various shades of brown and appeared very dry and devoid of vegetation. This was a harsh desert and beautiful in its own austere way. I remember thinking that this must be what the mountains of Tolkien's Mordor looked like. We were very far from home, and very much on our own.

Continuing north, the highway approached the Colorado River on the right which represented the border of California and Arizona. There was some green in those areas near the river, and there were agricultural areas established by irrigation from the river. Then the highway turned straight north away from the river and stopped at its perpendicular intersection with Interstate 10. Just west from there was the city of Blythe, near the border with Arizona. We found a KOA camp where we enjoyed a shower and washed our clothes. It was Halloween.

Arizona Up Hill

The next day we crossed the Colorado River and entered Arizona. Turning to the north off I-10 on Arizona State Highway 1, also called Mohave Road, we rode through a large agricultural area. The road followed the river which irrigated the vast fields of alfalfa and other crops. These lands belonged to Indian tribes. This was the Colorado Indian Reservation. Hwy 1 ended at Hwy 95 just south of Parker City. It was there that the irrigated farmlands ended, and a rough and rocky desert was on both sides. We camped that late afternoon next to a wash, which was a dry sandy riverbed. A sign warned of flash floods. There might be clear skies, but distant unseen rainstorms could cause a torrent of unexpected water and mud to come through. Other than that sign and the road, there was no other indication of civilization. The sun went down as Michael played his violin.

We continued north on Hwy 95 toward Lake Havasu, a large impoundment of the Colorado River. The stark mountains were devoid of vegetation and were colored in hues of dark brown and burnt orange. They were a great contrast to the blue lake below on our left. It was on this stretch that we encountered the first big storm of our ride. A great thunderstorm rolled in without warning in the middle of the day. We expected to make Lake Havasu City that afternoon, so we decided to continue. We tarped up, put our heads down and rode on thinking we could brave it but the wind was blowing hard. I can still see in my mind the lightning bolts striking the telephone and power poles right over our heads. The flashes of the lightning and the roar of the thunderclaps were simultaneous and caused me to flinch every time. There was nowhere to stop, no buildings anywhere, nowhere to shelter. It was a frightening situation! By the time we rolled into Lake Havasu City the storm was over. Those hours on the road seemed like forever. We were glad to find a KOA camp there where we could pitch our tent and dry out. Our mothers' prayers had been heard again.

Looking back after all these years, I am amazed at the endurance we had developed to be able to ride for so many hours each day. I wonder what my thoughts must have been as I put my head down and pedaled mile after mile into head winds and up endless hills. From Lake Havasu City to Kingman we climbed over 2600 feet in just 60 miles. From Kingman to Flagstaff we would climb 3552 feet in 150 miles. The western half of Arizona was one long gradual uphill run after another. You could see the mountain pass in the distance and once you finally reached it, a short downhill brought you to another long road that disappeared into the next mountain on the horizon. It seemed like every day brought a head wind. The western part of Arizona was hard work.

It was just past Kingman where we ran into trouble. North of Lake Havasu, Highway 95 ends into Interstate Highway 40 which runs east and then north to Kingman. At Kingman it turns back to the east and the long run to Flagstaff. This was the first time that we would be forced to ride for very long on an interstate highway. We were aware that bicyclists were not allowed to ride on them. Had there been a feeder road available we would have used it but there was no alternative. One day an Arizona State Highway Patrol officer stopped us. He explained how we were not allowed to ride on I-40. He pointed to a rocky dirt trail on the other side of the barbed wire fence that paralleled the highway. That trail would have destroyed our tires and rims in less than an hour. He was unsympathetic. He drove on. We waited a minute and rode on, via I-40. We had no choice. There was no other way east. We never saw him again, thank God, or any other peace officers. Well, not until much later, and for a very different reason.

As we made our way toward Flagstaff and gained altitude, the temperatures began to drop. It was early November, and we knew that the possibility of snowfall was near. We brought sufficient clothing to provide enough layering to be comfortable while riding and of course, our trusty goose down sleeping bags were a great blessing at night. I am not sure why, but I had neglected to bring any gloves. Riding into a cold breeze for hours had my poor hands practically frozen to the handlebars. In a town called Bellmont that is part of a Navaho reservation there was a small store where I was able to find a pair of pigskin work mittens that helped.

The High Desert

As the elevation increased and we neared Flagstaff, we began to see snow again. Riding on snow was not something that we wanted to experience on touring bike tires. We camped at a KOA camp in Flagstaff. This part of Arizona had beautiful pine forests and mountains which were a nice change from the high plains scrub that we had seen for days. Thankfully after Flagstaff we started a general descent on I-40 to Winslow and somewhat warmer temperatures. We were back on the high desert scrub. Winslow then was not like it is now. The song "Take It Easy" by the Eagles was only two years old then and its popularity had not found its way to the streets there yet. Nevertheless, we were excited to stand on a corner there for a minute (no sign of a girl my Lord in a flatbed ford), and even more excited to find a coin operated washateria that offered a shower as well. Traveling light as we were, you can just imagine how we and our clothing smelled after riding many hours a day for many days. Although we became accustomed to our unwashed condition, I found that the people who we came in contact with inside grocery stores and coffee shops were not very fond of our smell. Our clothing was covered in salt stains and our long hair and beards made us look like mountain men. I have clear memories of people backing away quickly on a grocery store aisle and women grabbing the hands of their young children! The Winslow wash was nice, but we were back on the road the next day and would not have another opportunity to cleanup for hundreds of miles.

Leaving Winslow on I-40, we continued heading east and then turned southeast on State Highway 180 at the small town of Holbrook. As we rode, we began to notice the colors of the roadside rock and gravel becoming richly red and orange. This vast desert area was once a forested land. Over time the trees had become covered and then fossilized. Now exposed to the weather they were broken down, creating the Painted Desert. About twenty miles down the road we came across the Petrified Forest National Park and the museum and lapidary shop there. The staff there invited us to set up camp and even share dinner with them. We enjoyed the fellowship and the food along with a tour of the beautiful, polished petrified wood tabletops that they created.

The next morning, I woke up deathly sick. I spent that day, and the next, crawling out of the tent to wretch on the ground with violent nausea and then back inside to collapse. Since no one else had become ill from the dinner, we imagined that I must have gotten a bad drink of water somewhere back up the road. Those were two miserable days in an uncomfortably warm tent. Although weak and worn out, I managed to mount up on the third day and we continued our ride.

Continuing south on 180, we passed through a town called St. Johns. We stopped in at a small store to buy some canned foods. This store also had silver and turquoise jewelry on display and for sale, which was so common in this part of the country. Continuing on, we camped as sun set approached. Looking at the map, we realized that we would be leaving Arizona and entering New Mexico the following day. It would be a long ride to Socorro, over 150 miles with few towns along the way.

The Law Catches Up With Us

The next day we stopped near the border in Springerville, at a gas station to fill our water bottles. While we were in the process of doing that, some cars pulled up and plain clothes Arizona State Police officers jumped out and confronted us. They searched us and ordered us to stand apart from our bikes a distance away in the parking lot without moving. While we stood there, they went through all of our belongings. They dismantled our bikes. They read our diaries. You can imagine our confusion and fear. After what seemed like hours, they began questioning us separately. They asked about our whereabouts and activities of the last two days. Eventually they were satisfied and explained what was going on. The small store in St. Johns where we had stopped to buy food had been robbed of their silver and turquoise jewelry and we were prime suspects. Why was never explained. They suggested that we leave Arizona and after re-assembling our bicycles and packing our gear, that's exactly what we did.

Blowing Through New Mexico

At nearly 7,000 feet of elevation, we continued east into New Mexico while a November cold front blew in. We reached a rest stop that was indicated on the map and there were several concrete picnic tables there. We made camp there for the night. The next morning while preparing breakfast, I spilled some water on the concrete tabletop and it froze instantly. We mounted up and pedaled on. I had to turn my face from side to side as numbness set in. Riding into a breeze increased the chill factor. The beard helped just a little bit. That was a long day on the road.

We crossed the Continental Divide near Pie Town and made it to Socorro in two days. I don't remember how it happened, but we were invited to stay in an old shelter in a junkyard by the old gentleman who owned it in Socorro. I was constantly on the lookout for scorpions and tarantulas in that old structure. The next day we turned south on Hwy 25 and then turned east on Hwy 380 towards Carrizozo with the White Sands Missile Range passing by on our right, riding some 75 miles. The next day we rode through the Capitan Mountains, the home of Smokey the Bear. In the town of Capitan there was a Smokey Bear Museum which we stopped to visit. That same day, we rode through Lincoln, and Hondo, which are in Apache and Billy the Kid country. Incredibly, we made it to Roswell just after dark, having pedaled some 90 miles. Some people that we had spoken with at the Smokey Bear Museum told us about what they called a "Christian flop house" in Roswell that would provide bed and a meal for travelers. We were able to find it, and they offered to put us up for the night. It was an old Victorian style house. The room that was provided to us had an old fashioned clawfoot bathtub. Our last opportunity to bathe had been a stand-up shower in the laundromat in Winslow. This was nearly 500 miles of riding and sweating later. After we had both had our turn to soak in this classic tub there was a thick ring on it.

They served us a dinner of macaroni and cheese with sliced hot dogs mixed in. It was good, like my mother used to make. Afterward, there was an invitation to attend a bible teaching. We passed on that invitation and I have come to regret that now. I was far from God in those days. It would be many years before that changed. Fortunately, even though we didn't know it at the time, we had our prayin' mothers. I know now that we had His protection during this adventure because of that.

The next day we headed south from Roswell to Carlsbad on Hwy. 285, a 76-mile ride. We had some excitement during that day's ride. The road was two lanes and it curved left just as an 18-wheeler, who had increased speed to pass another truck, came into our lane. The shoulder was narrow, and we had no choice but to dodge right and plunge down the steep gravel embankment. Thankfully, we managed to maintain control and stay in our saddles. Hearts pounding, we dismounted and pushed the bikes back up the embankment and continued our ride.

We wanted to visit Carlsbad Caverns. To do so, we needed to ride a short uphill road to White's City which is the tourist base for the caverns, some 20 miles. There we pitched our tent at a campground. I remember hearing snorting outside of the tent that night. It was always exciting to know that there was only a thin sheet of nylon between my face and a wild animal. I think that it must have been a javelina, a pig like animal of the desert.

We met a group of people at this campground

who offered us a ride the next day to get up to the caverns. We all decided to walk down through the caverns and take the elevator back to the surface. It was a truly amazing day. I managed to push back my claustrophobia enough to enjoy the caverns' beauty. I can still remember the musty smell of the huge piles of bat guano (poop) that had been laid down over thousands of years.

Breaking camp the next morning we headed back north to Carlsbad on the park highway and rejoined Hwy 285, called the Pecos Highway as it follows the Pecos River, and headed south toward Texas. We were now in the Chihuahuan Desert, the largest desert in North America, and we would be in it for a long time. The desert southwest is a huge place. Riding across it on a bicycle gives one a very personal understanding of that. I was humbled to think of how our pioneers managed to travel by horse, wagon, or on foot across it. The automobile has been a great advance in travel, but it has dulled our minds to the reality of the distance traveled. Air travel has done this even more so. In recent years as I have flown over the southwest on my way to California I have looked down and marveled at what it all looks like from 30,000 feet. It seems impossible to connect the two experiences: bicycle and airplane. What an amazing difference in perspective!

Texas, The Longest State

I remember clearly the day that we crossed the border into Texas. We stopped at a diner for pie and coffee. I was impressed by the waitress's Texan accent, the first we had heard. She was Texas friendly.

Following Hwy 285 we were now in a land where water planning was even more important. The distance between towns was becoming greater, sometimes more than 60 miles. About halfway between Fort Stockton and Sanderson we experienced a rash of broken spokes and flat tires. This was cattle country, somewhat hilly, rocky, and spotted with cactus, usually prickly pear. The only signs of civilization were the occasional windmills that pumped water into concrete tanks for the cattle.

A flat tire could be repaired quickly, but a broken spoke was another matter. The wheels of a bicycle need to be true. If not, there will quickly be problems, especially when carrying so much gear. By the time the repairs were made, there were not enough sunlight hours left to make it to Sanderson. We decided to pitch the tent on the other side of the barbed wire. We had become adept at lifting our bikes over the wire and then finding a place for the tent. There was a windmill visible up in the hills. We would use our water supply up that afternoon and then hike up to the cattle tank the next morning to refill our bottles, taking a chance that the water would not be contaminated. I sure did not want to go through that again, but there was no other choice. That hike up to the cattle tank the next morning turned out to be longer than it looked. We picked our way through the rocks and cactus and filled our bottles with the clean looking water in the concrete reservoir. Scrambling down and breaking camp, we were on our way toward Sanderson with no further setbacks. Nobody got sick from the water either.

We were on the Texas Pecos Trail, which would take us all the way to Del Rio before turning east across the center of the state. We were near the border with Mexico, following the Rio Grande which would join the Pecos River near Del Rio. This was wild west country. One of the great characters of the old west was Judge Roy Bean. He claimed to be "The Only Law West of the Pecos" and his court and home were in Langtry, TX, which is on the Pecos Trail between Sanderson and Del Rio. We stopped and enjoyed the museum there.

We were now very close to the Mexican border, the Rio Grande, and could see it at times. We crossed the wide Pecos River on a high bridge over a deep canyon cut by the river just south of where it joins the Rio Grande. Near Del Rio we stopped at a small store for supplies and learned that a storm was heading that way soon. The store had some hook ups and camping spots behind it, so we decided to rent one. Our small nylon tent had a rain fly that covered it to deflect water. We always pegged it down as securely as possible. That night it got a big test. After sundown, the storm rolled in with its powerful winds, great flashes of lightning, and ear-splitting thunderclaps. It's one thing to see the storm and ride through it. It's quite another to sit as an open target in the middle of it. Our tent was buffeted for hours but held firm. Our prayin' moms came through again! As the sun broke through the next day, we joined Highway 90 and headed east across the Great State of Texas. It would take many days to cross it. It's a big place.

Highway 90 would take us through many rural towns. This was ranching and farming land. We were leaving the Chihuahuan Desert and entering a vast agricultural expanse. This highway had a generous shoulder most of the time, which made riding much more comfortable and safer. It also had a number of rest stops where we would camp at times and call our moms. West Texas was well populated with deer and roadkill was common. Passing roadkill in a car is visually unpleasant. On a bicycle it is an olfactory nightmare. You just cannot hold your breath for very long while you are pumping those pedals!

On the east side of Uvalde, the sun was getting low and we decided to stop. Climbing up a small hill next to the road, we jumped the fence and made a hidden camp. Just across the road there was a honky tonk, so we decided to go over and visit. There was live country music playing so we stayed for a while and had a couple of beers. The drinking age in Texas was 18 back then. I was having a very hard time understanding what anyone was saying or singing. Now that I have lived in Texas for over 30 years, I easily understand everyone, but in those days "Texan" was a foreign language to me.

We approached San Antonio from the west side and passing Lackland Air Force Base, we first searched out the Alamo for a visit. It was right in the middle of the city and much smaller than I had imagined. Of course, nothing is ever the way they portray it in the movies! Then we pushed through the city and found a KOA camp where we could pitch our tent. The next day was Thanksgiving and we thought that it would be a good day to take a rest. We had not done that since Carlsbad Caverns. I bought a pint of whiskey and got lazy and Michael pulled out his fiddle. Salado Creek passed through the area and I did some exploring on foot.

Hwy 90 had joined Interstate 10 in San Antonio. We had done our best not to ride on the interstate highways but had no choice for a while. In Seguin, 90 diverged from I-10 in two directions. There was a road that tracked to the north of the interstate, and an alternate that tracked south of it. We chose the alternate and headed toward Houston. The weather was getting cooler, and some days we rode in the rain. I remember one particular day that was one of the best riding days of the whole trip. There was a consistent tail wind, and the terrain was gently hilly. The swales were perfectly situated so that we were constantly maintaining a good speed without struggle. The momentum gained from each downhill was equal to the power needed for the next hill. It was a cruising dream. We were back out in the ranch and farmland with wide shoulders and occasional rest stops available. Most of these had concrete tables and coverings and were built many decades before during the Great Depression.

I discovered a power lunch that worked well for igniting the afternoon ride. We would stop and buy a bunch of bananas and a couple of quarts of beer. I was always fueled up and ready to fly after that. We rode through Gonzales—famous for the cannon, Shiner—famous for the beer, Hallettsville, Eagle Lake, and then Rosenberg. Approaching Houston, we stopped just short and camped next to a small creek. We planned to visit Michael's aunt and uncle who lived north of Houston and thought that crossing this large city might be difficult. Getting back in the saddle the next morning, we continued on Alternate 90. Right away, we came across the Imperial

Sugar Plant. Later on, I would find out that this part of Houston was aptly called Sugarland. The plant is now a welcome center and museum. We picked our way through Houston that day. Many of the roads were full of potholes, and still are today. By the time we reached Mike's relative's home in Champions, my rear rim was ruined beyond repair. I would be unable to find a matching rim there in Houston and would have to settle for a heavier steel rim. My bicycle was never the same after that. We stayed there for a few days and were well taken care of. It was good R&R. I was not very impressed by Houston. It was very warm and humid during our visit and the destruction on my rear wheel did not help. Little did I know that I would move there many years later and would marry and raise a family there.

East Texas, Louisiana, and Lots of Swamp

Leaving the Champions area of Houston, Farm to Market Road 1960 took us east, and in Dayton joined Hwy 90 east toward Louisiana. This area of Texas was predominantly pine forest and water. The closer we got to Louisiana, the more water there was. This made finding campsites more and more difficult.

There were times that we would follow a gravel road off of the highway that would lead to a built-up area with an oil or gas well pump on it. There would be enough room there to pitch the tent, with swamp all around it. The pump equipment would come to life waking us from time to time in the night. There were other night sounds too. Swamp sounds that I didn't care to know too much about.

Highway 90 had us rejoin Interstate 10 in Beaumont, Texas, where the Neches River flows toward the Gulf of Mexico. I remember the bridge there and the maritime businesses along the river. We rode on toward the Louisiana border, which follows the Sabine River. Just before the border is the town of Orange. We had seen on the map that there was a rest stop on the outside of town and we planned to camp there. In Orange, there was a small diner on the highway. We stopped for coffee and a piece of pie. We asked the waitress about that rest stop that was up the road a few miles. She had more information for us than we had counted on, telling about how there had been a murder at that rest stop just the previous night. Someone had been killed there with a shotgun. We left knowing that we would have to camp there anyway, as there was nowhere else to go in that swampy land.

The sun was getting low as we rode into the rest stop. There was the usual drive around, and some picnic tables set well back with areas that had been used for camping. There was no one there. The shadows were getting long. Up went the tent and dinner was put on the camp stove. It had been another long ride that day. After a short time, a pick-up truck pulled off the highway and drove slowly through the drive around. It then got back on the road and drove away. A short time later it returned, turned in and stopped. Remembering what we had been told, I retrieved my Bowie knife. The driver got out and took a shotgun from the rack in his truck. He then started walking slowly towards us. There was nothing for us to do but wait. I gripped my knife. My heart was pounding. Time moved slowly. He walked past us and then down a trail that went on into the swamp land behind the rest stop. He was going hunting. Whew! Thanks again, Mom! I did not sleep well that night.

The next day we crossed the Sabine River Bridge and entered Louisiana. The highway straddled the great Tupelo Swamp. I remember the classic scenery it provided. Rural Louisiana was pine forest and swamp. The small towns, and farms rolled by. We had to be careful and skillful about locating our campsites, often having to climb fences which wasn't new. I remember stopping at a farmhouse to ask permission to pitch our tent on their land and not being able to communicate with the owners. They spoke a different language. Probably Cajun. There were flashlights nearby in the night which were probably hunters. Fortunately, we were never confronted. Stopping to buy provisions in small country stores we would ask about the road ahead. Sometimes the folks we spoke with had not been that far away before.

We passed through Lake Charles, Lafayette, and then Baton Rouge where we turned southeast on the Airline Highway which paralleled Interstate 10 and the Mississippi River on the way to New Orleans. A railroad track closely followed that highway, and we had to pitch our tent pretty close to it. Trains would roll by in the night and shake the ground like an earthquake. Sugar cane trucks would drive by us on the highway with overflowing loads, and we had to be careful to dodge the overboard canes on the road. Riding past the airport on our way onto New Orleans, we stopped at a park on the shore of Lake Ponchartrain and spoke with some people there who were curious about our journey. They told us about a woman who was known for offering shelter to travelers in her home. They showed us where she lived, and she very generously offered us shelter. We planned to stay a few days and explore New Orleans. We saw the French Quarter and other sights. I had my first "Hurricane" at Pat O'Brien's. After that we said goodbye and set our sights on Florida.

A Change in Plans

We got back on Hwy 90 and headed east, crossing through islands with many maritime businesses and then, on Hwy 11, a long bridge over the eastern end of Lake Ponchartrain. That brought us to Slidell where we stopped at a KOA camp for the night. The camp was busy, and some of the campers were heading west from Florida. We were running very low on funds and were counting on stopping in Florida to work and save up some money to continue our ride. These people assured us that there were few jobs available in Florida, which we had been hearing. We considered the facts. I was not happy with the steel rear rim that I had been riding on since Houston. It was sluggish and slow. We decided to return to New Orleans and find work. That wonderful lady who had put us up for a few days welcomed us back until we could get settled. Before long, we found an apartment on Carondelet one block off St. Charles and Louisiana in the Garden District of New Orleans. It was a large upstairs apartment with high ceilings and ceiling fans. At just one hundred dollars a month it was a God send. Prayin' Moms again! We both found jobs as telephone solicitors. It is funny that we both had tried that work back home in Los Gatos for a short time. We both did well at it. It did not pay very well but it was enough. I remember some of the radio hits at that time included The Doobie Brothers' "Black Water," and Elton John's cover of "Lucy In The Sky With Diamonds."

Michael enjoyed playing his fiddle with the street musicians in the French Quarter. I realized that my bicycle was not going to continue as a touring bike with that steel rear rim. There was no way that I would have been able to afford a new one. In addition, it would be impossible to save enough money to continue the adventure. At one point some street friends made us aware that Tulane University Medical School was looking for people to take part in the testing of a new antibiotic drug for which they would receive $300. I decided to go ahead with it so I could afford a train ticket home. Participants were required to collect their urine in a large white plastic bottle, and their poop in a plastic bag, and bring them to the downtown campus every week. This would mean carrying my "samples" on the streetcar and leaving my bottle and bag at my desk at work every day. Thank God that's not how it's done now! But by the end of May, I was able to buy an Amtrak train ticket that would take me back home to the Bay Area.

Home Again

Heading back home on a train was somewhat surreal. One of the most amazing adventures of my life had come to an end. As I watched the swamps, southwestern deserts and the coast of California speed by the windows of the train car, I marveled at how, in two days on a train, I covered the territory that had taken us over three months to conquer by bicycle. There was disappointment that we had not been able to go farther on our journey. Even still, I knew that I was coming back with a confidence gained from a great test. A test of perseverance. Michael stayed in New Orleans for some time and gained experience with the musicians there that I am sure benefit him to this day. When I got off of the train in San Jose, my mother, father, and brothers were waiting there on the platform. They all had big smiles. My father said that I looked like Jesus with my long hair and beard, and we enjoyed a laugh as we headed home.

Since those days, I have been thankful for the perspective and sense of proportion that this adventure provided me. Our world is a far bigger place than we are often led to believe. As a child, my family traveled by car across the USA several times and it had given me an appreciation for the size of the United States of America, but this journey really brought it home. Thinking about how much our ancestors had to do to conquer these vast territories is humbling. We had nice bicycles and roads to follow. They often did not even have a clear trail. There were no gas stations or food stores or pay phones. But I am sure that, like us, they had prayin' mothers too.

All these years later, I have come to truly appreciate what my mother's prayers did for me. I understand now that it was not by my own strength that I survived and returned. In 2005, I came to know the God my mother prayed to. I made the decision to accept Jesus as my Lord and Savior and that's when the greatest adventure of my life began—a spiritual adventure. It too has had some twists and turns, difficulties, and unexpected moments but to feel truly alive—it is all worth it. I can thank my mother's prayers for that too.

If your heart is longing for adventure, for freedom, for something more, I can bet someone has been prayin' for you. Let me encourage you to open yourself up to the ride of your life—a personal relationship with Jesus' Christ. It's really very simple and there isn't any preparation involved. Just take a moment and invite Him into your life. Be willing to surrender all to Him and He will take you on an epic spiritual journey.

If you are a prayin' mother or father or grandparent or friend, let me encourage you, don't stop. You never know how far someone is going to ride away from home before they come back again. I thank God for those who have gone before me, for those who stood by, and those who mentored me, but when I look back over my life and consider this journey, most of all I thank God we had prayin' mothers.

Michael and me at a rest and maintenance stop.

Michael and me packed up and ready to continue our ride. I am
wearing the leather headband that Pamela made for me.

Michael and me packed up and ready to leave from my parents'
house in Los Gatos, CA. that first day in September, 1994.

Heading out from my parents' house on Elwood Dr. the morning of the first day.

The two lane highway heading east through the Anza Borrego Desert in Southern California.

ABOUT THE AUTHOR

Dr. Neal Robinson lives in Houston, Texas with his wife Elaine. He has a chiropractic practice and is a professional fitness instructor. He and Elaine conduct a homeless ministry and they both serve at Lakewood Church. Dr. Neal still rides his bicycle!

PUBLISH & GO PRESS
H O U S T O N

Jacket design and interior layout by Chris Boyer.

Visit our website at www.PublishAndGo.com

9 781735 588346